Pitt Poetry Series

Ed Ochester, Editor

On Foot,
in Flames

Robert McDowell

UNIVERSITY OF
PITTSBURGH PRESS

The publication of this book
is supported by a grant from the
Pennsylvania Council on the Arts.

Published by the University of Pittsburgh Press,
Pittsburgh, Pa., 15260

Copyright © 2002, Robert McDowell

Manufactured in the United States of America

Printed on acid-free paper

10 9 8 7 6 5 4 3 2 1

ISBN 0-8229-5783-3

CONTENTS

Four

Five

ON FOOT, IN FLAMES

The harvest is the end of the age
and the harvesters are angels.

—*Matthew 13:39*

Where and What You Are

I see you in a hundred places. Now
You've gone into the writing where anything
Can happen, and nothing is still. If you know
A shortcut to the flesh, a sweet sighing
From the souls of trees that we might make our own
Just say it, so. At least tonight the moon
Is confident. The riverbed is wet
From a summer squall. Tonight I'll make a bet
With you. I'll wager that the hands that tear
The living from the writing disappear,
As will the distance that is like too many
Clothes between us. Braver, unafraid,
You are a light that calms and covers me.
You own me now that you are everywhere.

ONE

I saw so much before I slept there once . . .

—*Robert Frost, "The Mountain"*

The Valley of the In-Betweens

Nobody knows the moon as it used to be.
None of us hears a thing:
Not the singing to Christ at evening mass,
Not the joy of sex from the leather room,
Not the scythe of triumph whispering over the field.
Nobody sees the sun, or the light
Spilling weakly under the locked door.
Deaf, blind, too much alone, we
Are late, fearing the feeling of fear
As we tremble in the draft of a high,

Open window, as we sigh at dusk,
As we hide from the mad celebration
Down in the street. At the point
Of the draw is a bubble of blood
That hesitates in rounding the curve of a vein.
In the skull is a cloud,
In the chest is a barn.
Between you and the sticks you must use
To build your house stands a bird of prey,
And a hunter's red eye in the dark.

The New Life

Dandy walked out of his closet a new man.
The prescription drugs were working,
As were the sessions with Ms. K.
At last he had overcome his urge
To be eating all the time (especially
the ice cream quarts before bed).
Now his fat clothes were shoved
Aside, his thin clothes bunched
Toward the front by the closet door.
His feet at least were constants, so
His shoes stayed the same, as did
His relatives, though not his friends.
He would be seeing less of his eating friends,
And those he had come to think of as
The drones of Ms. K. They made
A great display of checking in, though
All their talk about *Dandy's* feelings were
Prefaces to lingering discourses on their own.

His first week out of the center,
Dandy drove all over the city. After that
He spent a lot of time in bed, planning things.
Maybe he would make some contribution,
Especially to those less fortunate than he.
He thought about moving to the country.
The refrigerator's spiritual hum made him think
About tearing through all-you-can-eat buffets,
And he thought about following Ms. K.
He thought about climbing to some high spot
Where only the wind could reach him,
Where the puzzle pieces far below
Would settle into place, just as they should be.

At Home with Dollface

I stepped down into the little cardboard town.
All day and night we were posing.
I did not need to water or cut
Our plastic lawn, and I gave up shaving because
In my beloved's world no hair or green thing grew.
My teeth were exquisitely white,
My body fat absolutely zero.
We dressed from wardrobes without end,
And drove our pink convertible to the river each day.

One might think that we yearned for some controversy,
A little spice mixed into the bland stew of our days.
In fact, we were deliriously happy, content with our clothes
And gadgets, determined to look out
At the world's woe through the wise eyes of toys.

Chug's Promise

Chug never held it against his wife
That they married because she was pregnant.

He squandered his pay on the horses
Because he wanted to take her to Europe.

He kept his wife from the baby who cried
All night insisting she get some rest.

He slept with his sister-in-law,
Having seen it once in a movie.

He lost his job because his boss was jealous,
Then he bruised one side of his wife's face for love.

He threatened to take the children away forever,
Fearing the lawyers would soak up all their savings.

Then he drove them over the state line
And called her from a phone booth outside Lincoln.

He said he was putting the bad times behind him,
That she could join them when he got on his feet.

He promised to send money and photos of the kids.
Crying, he told her he couldn't talk anymore.

He said he'd call later when they were settled.
He said they'd all be happy. Just like they used to be.

The Fleshing Machine

Their deaths, we're told, are quick, painless.
From saltwater baths their hides
Are stacked on the beam house floor.
Forklifts flick out their tongues
And bring them to where we work the foot
Pedals that open and close the great mouths.

Stitched into gloves and apron,
Lye-spattered, soaked with grease,
I feed my machine 1,200 hides a day.
Sometimes I think *this was the neck, this the tail.*
The man I replaced
Paid for his carelessness with an arm.

The break room minutes drip through the pores of a dartboard.
Back at it again, I savor the codeine kicking in.
All day I keep turning, lightheaded,
Toward the loads of dead weight,
Then round to my dumpster
Filling with hides stripped clean.

When the whistle blows, before day is done,
I hose down and floss the giant's teeth.
Some days I curse Jesus
Because money has become my only Book.
Some days I thank Him
For having this job, my daily bread.

There Is

In certain Oregon rivers the fish are dead;
Another beautiful stand of trees is cut.
But there is also the morning air,
The new-mown, harrowed field turning
Green, after early rain, in the late fall sun,
And horses nickering for alfalfa when
You first appear at the barn door,
Singing for the lame mare.
There is the tree house under construction,
The barn itself forever under repair.
There is still, for all its shadows,

The familiar light of home, its voices
Comforting from other rooms,
And the children on their way to school.
And there is always the calendar, not simply
Telling you another living day is through,
But igniting recollections of the days when you
Surprised yourself with competence, even grace.
There is blue ink on a cream-colored page,
A blue heron, imperious, commanding
The pond. And there is always you:
What you choose to believe and do.

Surprise

It's sad, the woman thinks, who has heard it all
Before: The celebration of her breasts,
Her eyes bright suns or moons, her hair so brash,
The grace of her egret neck, his grateful voice
More like a rushing wave—it is so full—
Than calm consideration of her gifts.
And so she settles back, a motel dove,
And takes her time pulling on her socks.
She's mad, she tells herself, to fall for this
Again, but there is so much hunger in
The way he looks at her. It might be love.
Weighing odds, the things they'll do today,
She leans, as to a whetstone, her sickle-self
To sharpen their future, or grind it all away.

My Bird, Your Face

You'd be surprised. I've trained my bird to sound
Your voice. If I could will each face I meet
To be your face, I'd spend more time in public
Instead of in this room, with only the bird
For company. I keep the curtains closed
And go out when the alarm clock tells me to.
I work a graveyard shift. Unable to
Maintain a car, I ride the bus to work.
You see, what time I've left I put behind
Me since that night you cut me open through
The telephone. I'm happy just to sit here,
Unrecognizable to all but the bird,
Ever faithful, greeting me as you
Used to do: *Hello, darling. Hello, darling.*

Lower Levels

At times she is
so lost to him
he cannot find
her even in
a chair across
the room. She sits
so far away
he asks himself,
how do I know
this traveler
who goes alone,
this one-way fare,
this partner who,
on any day,
might fly away
forever from
the farm? A star-
gazer withers
in a jar on
a windowsill.
The vineyard freezes,
the orchard, too.
Who lives without
attention, or
survives too much
of it? The books
of happy end-
ings mock them well.
So this is Heaven, so this is Hell.

Levels of Intersection

Rain plows into the Willamette, rushes on.
A young man at a rest stop along I-5
Leans against his Ford Fairlane, smoking.
The sky is robin's egg blue, breaking through
Peaks and funnels of white clouds so immense
That giants might be hiding out in them,
Or throwing parties, or holding election rallies.
Maybe the man travels in a dream of love and money,
Driving to reunion or renewal.
And even if his heart is aching from the company
Of the radio, his journey is not forever,
His uneasiness a momentary weather.
Is that the memory of his mother's kiss
He puts away, the distant look in his father's eye?
Stubbing out his cigarette, does he see
Some welcome waiting for him north of here?

Now take away projection, the things we see
In others that are really just ourselves.
That leaves us with a young man in a Fairlane
Driving away under a clearing Oregon sky.
Who knows what he may be running from or
Driving to? Our intersection fixed the time, one day.
We saw him on his way somewhere, perhaps
To do somebody dirt, perhaps to repair.

My Eastern Friend

When he was young he lived for drama.
He wished himself in a French movie,
Exchanging intellectual, sexist dialogue
With beautiful European women.
One by one, he took girls on long drives
Through the countryside in his two-seater.
Even under threatening skies he
Kept the top down. "For the romance,"
He said, "for the drama."

None complained. They drove
To get wet, to feel the wind set
Their hair on end, to feel the elements
On their skin like hands all over them.
"Baby," they called each other, and "Toots."
They were dollfaces, sweethearts.
Be it rain, be it sweat, it was wetness
They were after, long days and nights of it,
The romance of it.

At forty my friend gave up drink
And got heavy. "It's a shame
That drinking, and the loss
Of drinking, inhibit the drama," he said.
He slapped at his belly, insisting
That touching it was like setting one's hand
Unexpectedly in warm gum. To his credit,
He did this as if he were waving a flag.

Driving home from an AA meeting,
My friend was in a talkative mood.

"I laid down with so many," he said,
"I grew weary (appreciative, but weary).
I lived the drama, discovering romance.
But lately I find I remember more clearly,
And worship more dearly, the flawed bodies,
The wrinkled, the whittled, the scarred
And varicose-veined, the overweight,
The thinned out, the lovers haunted
By everything but perfection.
These defined romance,
Having many miles of it on them."

❧

My friend, approaching fifty, grows quiet,
Though a mutual acquaintance assures me
He is only turning up the volume elsewhere.
I hope so. I could not stand to think
Of his car up on blocks in some garage,
His fire put out by the torrent of so much drama,
That from now on I must miss him,
My cohort, my spy, my chronicler of romance.

Sisters

Diana wakes up in a Motel Six,
Pulls back the musty curtain from a window
In an upstairs single room and snaps her gum.
She sees the driveway to and from the road,
The reflection of her face, and circles back
To the reservation—leaving it with Rose
To open a quilt and linen shop in Barstow.
Their hard-luck mother jeered at them while Dad
Just popped a Coors and looked the other way.

Jump on a crack and break your mother's back

The two girls sang that night on the Barstow bus,
But no Cinderella ending met these two.
A little more than a month had ticked away
And business, as one might expect, was going slow.
One Friday Rose was sweeping out the shop
When who but Dad slammed in, a wobbly, lethal
Sack of beer and bitterness.
                              "Money,"
He said. "You owe me and I want my cut.
Don't sass! Your mother's waiting in the car."

Beyond his shoulder Rose could see her there,
Talking to herself, arguing really,
And then and there she knew what she would do.

"We ran away because we hated home,
And me more than Diana hated you.
You want to feel me up? Get mean like last
December when I made a break for it?"

The man was breathing heavy, moving slow,
And with one hand he loosened up his belt.
"I run this family," he said, "like always.
You need to be reminded, little girl."
Rose backed behind the counter, groping for
An object she could drive into his head
Or heart, anything to stop him with.

Adrenalin disguised the alcohol
And made him feel like a boxer on a roll.
And that's just how he moved. He clubbed her with
A fist across the mouth, smashing past
The broom she raised to spear him with, then helped her up
So he could grin and knock her down again.
Before the woman in the car out front
Could reason through the evil things the voice
Inside her head was saying, the man in the store
Had touched their daughter Rose for one last time.
She died on the cold floor of that small shop
Without regaining consciousness to tell
Her killer where she and her sister roomed.
If she'd come to, she would have spit in his face
Before she told him anything of use.
He rifled through her clothes, of course, coming
Up with seven dollars and some change.
He searched the back but couldn't find her purse,
Then tapped the register and hit the street.

The woman rocking in the passenger seat
Did not look over as he scooted in.
He punched the Chevy through a U-turn east

And stared off like a bulldozer at the road.
"Come out of it," he said.
                              His wife spoke up.
"What'd you do back there? It's bad. I hear
It in your voice. Were you mean to baby Rose?"

The driver sped up then to squash a mouse
That skittered from the stubble of a field.
"I didn't mean to hit her like I did,"
He said at last. "I figured she was faking,
You know, so's not to have to come across.
But then she wouldn't hear me or get up."
The terror rising in his voice and face
Poured out and made the cabin feel too small.
The nagging, inside voice the woman fought
With day and night was gone. Instead, she felt
A stabbing point of light ram through her head
And wipe out any sense of a past life.
She knew again how it looked to wake up dead
And didn't feel a thing when he touched her arm.
"We'll have to drive real hard all night," he said.
A bloated, empty moon undressed the road.

        The investigation entered its third month
When Diana closed the shop for good, took all
Her savings from the bank and bought a car
To track them down like two dumb animals.
Through Oregon and Washington she drove,
Then backtracked south through Portland. Turning east
She left the forest coastal land behind,

Attacked the arid plains of Idaho,
With Utah next if hunting came to that.

She stopped at reservations on her way,
But never came on news of two doomed people
Running from their past. Good company
Was all she got, and that would make her soft.
She had a vengeful spirit guiding her,
And she took care to feed it every hour.
"When I closed our shop, I closed my future, too,"
She'd tell police—but that would be awhile.
She had to find them first.
                                    Then in McColl
She saw them coming out of a convenience store.
She broke into a sweat, then thought of Rose
And calmed herself enough to follow them
Until they stopped at this motel. Diana
Watched them as they climbed to 23,
And noticed how they both looked bowed and sick.
She told herself *when guilt and fear stew in*
One pot the eaters thin out day by day.
Then she took a room herself and fell asleep.

    Now through the parted curtains as the sun
Comes up, she sees the fugitives packing the car.
Squashing out her cigarette she takes
A bundle from her purse and tears the paper
Away to load the .38 she bought
With Rose's final cut.
                              That's justice, she thinks,
But now she loads the gun, her mind a blank.

Down in the parking lot, her mother sees
Her first, though what she sees is like a dream.
"It's Rose," she says as natural as if
Her little girl were skipping down the road
From the school bus.
                    Diana lifts her arm
And waits for the man, condemned, to turn around.
Freezing as his wife speaks first he stays,
Then crouches down and runs. Diana drops
Him with one shot. His face down in the brush,
He goes out instantly without a thought.

"You gonna shoot me now?" her mother asks.
Diana cocks the gun, bites through her lip
And lets her gun arm fall.
                        "I'm settled now,"
She says. "Who needs a father, or a mother?
Let's sit down, just the two of us, and wait."

The Red Ball

Everywhere I go it follows me.
Not long ago I said, at a table of eight,
That I would never feel so much again.
Just then the rough, red sun infected us
Through the picture window.
                           Oh, lighten up!
Our hostess said, more nervous than amused.
Before I made apologies I said
You won't find me above the crowd again,
Or levitating others, or in the field
Amusing children with my roping skills.

The others, who'd had enough, were glad to see
Me go. I nodded, bowed, and tried to soften
The sound of my clicking boot heels on the floor.
Behind me, rounded faces flushed as if
On fire, while in the yard the hitching post
Had changed into a circle and rolled away.
And so it was I found myself on foot,
In flames, so far away from you I did
Not care that I must walk up one side of
The burning ball, or stumble down the other.

TWO

And I said, let grief be a fallen leaf
at the dawning of the day.

—*Patrick Kavanagh, "On Raglan Road"*

The Pact

Rain bulled into the valley like a giant
Escaping from the pages of a book.
John-Allen in his garden watched it brawling
Over the coastal range. Its highest peaks
Gleamed briefly in the sun that broke above
The Cascade Mountains fifty miles to the east,
Then disappeared in swirling thunderheads.
Behind him his blue house reflected deeper blue
As all the valley darkened, and the wind
Coming in warm gusts that flattened the grass
Advanced on the pear tree, then on himself.
His straw hat blew off, flew crazily away,
Splitting the wicket of two apple trees
Before hanging up suddenly among the roses.
John-Allen still faced west, his hair straight back,
His eyes tearing. He knew he should go in
But tightened his grip on the fence. The storm inside
Would outlast this one, which was beautiful.
A moment's silence, then thunder came calling,
Then all the fury of the storm broke loose.

John-Allen let the rain wet down his face.
He saw the dust on leathery leaves explode,
A grasshopper dive for cover in the grass.
He heard the plastic pinging on raised beds,
And saw her at the back door, under the awning,
Looking out for him, or admiring the storm.
He didn't know which, or care, he told himself.
It hurt to look at her, to get up close.
She stepped aside, her eyes still on the storm.
John-Allen stopped, as if to go in alone

Meant he would lose her for good.

Already lost,

He thought. He wanted her to go, and stay.
The rain he tramped in stained the worn fir floor.
He hung his slicker up. "Your packing done?"
She sighed, but only the storm would answer him.
He stared into the coil of yellow hair
She always bunched and pinned when she was working;
His head grew light. He grabbed the door for balance.
It's then she looked at him.

"Are you all right?"

"This rain has given me a chill," he lied.

She turned back in, their bodies almost touching,
His shoulder leaning toward her, but obstinate.

"Come in. The fire's stoked, the kettle's on."

His body tingled, polished and alert
From where she touched his arm above the elbow.
He stepped out of his boots and toweled off.
She poured out tea. He trembled as he drank.

"You're shaking," she said, as one might say *you're fine*,
Mixing reassurance with the fact.
He forced another swallow, burning his tongue,
Insisted he'd be all right with a change of clothes.
"I'll get them for you."

"No, don't bother," he said.

Upstairs he found her suitcase on the bed,
Still open, as if still weighing in the balance.

Her folded flannel nightgown, lying on top,
Distressed John-Allen so his breath got short.
He reached for the inhaler and sat down;
One shot and he was breathing easier.
He touched the nightgown, tracing with his finger
The pattern of embroidery at the neck.
He put his face to it and breathed her in,
Then started at the imagined scent of hay
Turning his reluctant mind to memory,
To the night he pulled in early, noticing
The burned-out light, the darkness on the porch,
The darker stillness of the house, its calm
Unbroken by him calling Sarah's name.
He unpacked papers, put away his clothes,
And sat up hours beside the telephone.
At two he went to bed, the cat at his feet.
Near dawn the crunch of gravel woke him up.
He listened to the key click into place,
The door creaking on its hinges, then clapping shut.
John-Allen at the window saw the truck,
The driver hesitating, then moving on
While up the stairs behind him she appeared.
He turned to bloodshot eyes above the circles,
The pale skin even lighter than it was
When she was rested. Her eyes told everything.

"You're early." (Sarah began with the obvious.)
He stood his ground, endured the flash of options,

The swift steps closing the distance between them,
His hand, as if another's, flaring up
And sparking in its fury as it crashed
Into her upturned, unresisting face.
He could see her body tense to take the blow,
Her nerves all bunched together to absorb
His rage should it break free and burn through her.
Denying the release of a moment's violence,
John-Allen said no word. Her face grew crimped
And even paler; her straining body sagged.
That gave him satisfaction. He almost smiled,
Then felt like weeping for the sickness in it.

In a moment she came downstairs after him,
Trying to bridge the awful awkwardness
Between them with a flurry of routine,
But as the coffee beans ground down, his question
Vibrated in her as if she were a bell.
"How long?" was all he said, not *who*, or *why*.

A knot of raw emotions writhed in her—
Amusement, anger, defiance, even remorse—
Then broke out in a rush of laughing tears.
John-Allen waited for the fit to pass
And stared out at the field where a cloud of birds
Descended, ravenous, pecking the ground
Then swarming up en masse and moving on.
He thought them lucky, all of a single mind,
And knew no humans could ever live like that.
As Sarah calmed herself he studied her,
The way she jabbed at her eyes with a paper towel

And wiped her reddening nose, stuffed up and swollen.
He pitied her, then steeled himself against it.
They sat down with their coffee, fingered their cups,
Their talk taking shape reluctantly at first
Then shifting back and forth between two poles—
One brimming with aggression, the other restrained.

Inside them there were voices talking, too.
John-Allen's needled him:
                              What'll you do?
You could kill the lover, your wife, even yourself;
You could stay with her, or go on alone.

But how? The thought of starting over ached;
Forgiveness seemed a saintly, distant thing
Beyond his reach.
                    The woman wrestled, too,
With what her private voice was telling her.

Before he knew, just one long day ago,
You found a tension you had dreamed about.
Now you must choose: follow it away
Or stay here if you can. You've loved each other,
You've built this house, you've shared a history.

"We built this place," she said, as if prompted to speak.
"If you won't talk, if you won't help me now,
I'll have to make out what you mean myself.
Please look at me!" She shook him by the shoulder,
Surprising him with her strength. Like one asleep
John-Allen moved. The subtlest counterpressure

Was enough to render each one motionless.
But still he did not speak.
                         "I can't explain,"
She said, "why I went out behind your back.
The boy's no older than my younger brother,
Not yet a man. He acted so clumsy at first,
But he kept me company. He helped me out
Those six weeks you were driving Idaho.
Why did we cross the line? I can't be sure.
I guess I felt—I don't mean to sting you
By saying this—as if I were on vacation,
As if we were taking a break from all this . . . *life*
We've put together. It didn't mean I quit.
I'll tell you, John, the shine came back to us
The more I saw us from far away. It's then
I knew I loved you as I always had.
Now tell me if that means we can't go on."

The sun came up, squeezing the chill from the air.
By noon a yellow haze distorted the light
As seed grass farmers scorched their acreage.
The cows in Frazier's field roamed far to graze,
Then ambled back to the sheds by four o'clock.
A good burn day, they called it in the valley,
A day to stay indoors. John-Allen and Sarah
Had nowhere else to go. They sat talking together,
Reaching the point where nothing new came up,
But neither wished to put an end to talk
For fear that if they stopped they'd never start.

🌾

Not far from there the lover wired himself
On bitter truck stop coffee. All day he trembled
Between his seat and the phone by the register.
His coins exploding on the metal tray
Provoked a glare from the girl behind the counter.
Each time she settled into a hostile boredom
Broken only by curt efficiency
When someone slapped a ticket on the glass.
The sounds of talk and eating buzzed in his mind,
And no call he made got through, not to his boss
To say that he would not be in to work,
Not to his mother, who dozed on beer in her hammock,
Not to Sarah, whose line was busy or off the hook.
He thought of her denying both of them
(A young man's fear of betrayal is like no other's).
He wanted to confess, confide in someone,
But being true he'd kept this to himself.
Had Sarah named him? He shivered at the thought.

Just after five the dinner crowd began
To straggle in—farmers mostly, eating alone,
Or in twos or threes, a few with families.
These last ones hurt the most.
                              Too many people,
The boy decided. Were they watching him,
Some even laughing at his foolishness?
He paid his check and drove his truck due east
To the winding gravel spur of Enos Lane,
Which led him to just a field away from her—
Her property, at least—or was it the man's?

He'd never asked.
The valley smoke had settled
By dusk, though some black flakes of ash still floated
Like apple or cherry blossoms on gusts of air.
One landed on his shoulder—a star? An omen?
But he was much too literal for that.
He kept to the line of scrub oak, disturbing sheep
That feasted in the shade of the blackberry thicket.
He willed his cough away as he drew near
The barn's back door. It opened soundlessly.
He stepped inside involuntarily thrilled,
Imagining that Sarah was waiting there
To stun him with a look of mock surprise
Then move up close, inviting him to touch.
The smell of her hair, the feel of her moist skin
Beneath the summer dress that fell away
So easily, his own clothes slipping off—

But that was all over now. The sick light splashed
across the sagging floor, and no one came.
The boy stood swaying from the shock of loneliness;
He shut his eyes, attempting to calm down,
Then knelt by the tractor, picking apart an owl pellet.
A starling's indigestible beak and bones
Repulsed and fascinated him. If only
He had made the difficult connection there,
That all life turns on bursts and fits of passion
Leaving behind a clump of broken bones,
A slimy trail, a smear on a patch of earth.
He was wounded, though still too inexperienced
To know all stains are beautiful, sure signs

That life has happened.
                              But the boy could only wish
That Sarah would find him there. Yet she'd promised nothing
(How could she? They had so little to talk about.)
And kneeling on that floor of hardened dung
He muttered angrily, then took it back,
His mind refusing to cooperate
With cursing her when all it anchored on
Were images of love. He pitied her,
But much more himself, and peered through slats at the house.
He thought of rushing in to rescue her,
Then heard again her voice admonishing:

Whatever happens, you cannot interfere.

Did she know her command had circumscribed his life,
That he'd take her at her word? His future closed.
The hackamore fell softly over the beam
Above his head, the noose efficiently tightened.
The body, calming, swung so rhythmically
An animal watching might easily fall asleep.

              Past dusk, John-Allen rolled the huge doors back
And held his breath at the slow revolving motion
Of the body above. He heaved the poor boy down
And checked his pulse, though he knew death when he saw it.
He knew the boy, yet in his shock he missed
The obvious, the rapid steps behind him.
Then Sarah's moaning covered all of them—
The solid, hardened man above the boy,

Herself keening in sickly afterlight.
John-Allen laid the corpse on a bed of hay
And firmly pressured Sarah from the barn.

Later, they talked in the frightened voices of children.
By midnight they had calmed their nerves with drink,
Measuring what to do. Should they call police?
They'd have to leave the valley, and it would ruin
The dead boy's memory; his mother would break,
The locals would be cruel.
                              Toward sun-up he said,
"It's our affair, or I should say it's been yours.
I'm game to keep it here, but you should go.
We'll say you've gone back east to see your people.
Folks will gossip, wondering where you are,
But that'll pass. In time they'll just ignore it."

"But what about now?" Sarah's voice was thin.
He knew she meant the body in the barn.

"We'll lay him down in the addition," he said,
"Back by the window. Then we'll pour a slab.
I'll dig, and you can read the Scriptures over him."

She stood as if on cue and got the Book.
John-Allen fetched his gloves, his knee-high boots,
And single file they marched to the gloomy barn
Where they made quick work of it. With an owl as witness
John-Allen gently laid the dead boy down.
Removing his cap and gloves, he bowed his head
And listened fiercely to the 23rd Psalm.

🌿

The next day's weather broke out cold and clear.
A midnight wind had gusted through the pass,
Pushing the field smoke north to Washington.
On other days like this they'd feel refreshed,
The valley clean, themselves primed for renewal,
But today bore all the weight of what they'd done.
As Sarah scrambled eggs that neither would eat,
John-Allen stared out at the fields and barn,
The coffee getting colder in his mug.
I'll stay with you . . . her words kept playing him,
But to what march? The blind steps of a fool?
He struggled with his pride, despising Sarah
And hating himself for not forgiving her.
So far he had survived the thing she'd done,
And would, most likely. She asked for a little time;
That suited him. He said he'd wait a month.
That night he made his bed up in the attic.
Above her Sarah heard John-Allen pacing.
A month would pass so quickly. Where would she go?

In half that time the weather turned to snow
And rain that made the people speak of Noah.
The valley lay unconscious under a cloud
Of cold that penetrated everything.
The creaking out of beds, the straightening up,
The numbing of cold and sleep-entangled minds
Made every morning thick and difficult.
Even so, the valley farmers worked
Their fields in heavy gear. Who prayed for rain
In August now prayed as hard for an end to rain,

For any rip in the horizon's shawl
Of unrelenting gray.
                    John-Allen heard
Some mention of the boy, a question or two
At grange or auction block that tweaked his heart,
But the talk gave way to the waitress's engagement,
The cashier's shame (exposed for tapping the till),
The Lower MacKenzie's polluted salmon run,
And long debates about the spotted owl
Or methods to make burning obsolete.
The boy, some figured, was done in by a drifter,
While others thought he'd simply moved away.
His mother drank more beer, and that was that.

But not for them. Their lives were like a recording
Playing over and over. Their grief was their own.
Sarah forced herself to look ahead,
So each day, with eagerness and manic cheer,
She cooked fine meals and kept a spotless house,
Helped out in the fields if there was need of it
Yet always avoided the barn.
                              He noticed that
But didn't speak of it. *That's natural,*
He thought, himself finding fewer occasions
To go in there. He kept his distance in all ways,
Working the fields more than he had before
Or parking his tractor to watch the stars at night,
Though nothing he read there made living easier.
Or more to the point, showed him *how* to do it.
Then one day after supper she told him
The time had come. In the morning he could drive her

To the train in Albany. From his bed in the attic
He heard the opening and closing of drawers.

❦

The day had come. He kept her waiting with work
Outside until the weather drove him in.
Now he lay beside the suitcase on the bed
And touched its spine. His eyes burned in the dark.

So this is what your pride has made of you,
He told himself, *companion to misery.*
What difference does it make? She cheated you
But otherwise stuck by you. She's tried her best
To make amends, and you've been touched by that
In spite of yourself, and now this further bond
Between the two of you that can't be broken.
What's natural or evil between two people?
You want and need each other. Let it go.

The door half-opened. Sarah hesitated,
Then spoke uncertainly.
                                    "John-Allen, it's time."

He couldn't speak. She waited a moment longer,
Perhaps for the suitcase to levitate and float
As in a Disney movie, to her hand.
The silly image faded. She reached for the bag,
And as she closed her fingers on its handle
His own hand, haltingly at first, found hers.
She held her breath, her husband did the same,
And then both hands gripped harder, holding on.
Now nothing was held back, not even words,

As Sarah lay beside him in his arms.
Outside the sky was calm above the farm,
Though to the north the rain had turned to hail.
Over the coastal range a new storm blew.
The fall was ending. Winter had begun.

THREE

Allegiance to the land is tenderness.

—*Maxine Kumin, "Hay"*

After

Now morning comes. The air at last is warm,
And sleep is gone from your eyes. Turn out the light,
The one you read by, that stayed with you all night,
And step into the world. Silence your alarm.

Turn out the light and look out on the farm
Where wind stirs up the leaves and the trees repair.
"Come down to me in your cloud of raven hair,"
You hear yourself repeating like a charm,

But the one you're thinking of is in a dream.
Protect her there, and everywhere, you pray.
The one you love is elsewhere, so far away
Her absence shapes the night into a scream.

Yet morning comes, and though its hours endure
The calendar full of everything but her,
May they also ease your troubles, carry you far,
Safely, maybe even back to her.

October

He hung his yellow slicker on a hook
And skimmed the moisture from a windowpane.
A horse looked through his gaze and shook off rain,
Ignoring cows that lumbered through the gate
Like swaying movie stars oblivious
To common measurements of loss and gain.

He wondered where the one true ledger lay—
Inside a cloud, a drawer, an orderly head?
Alone among the commerce of the beasts
He wished that God would coax them into speech.
"Come out and shimmy-shammy with our kind,"
He heard them call through snorts and coughs of steam,

But only in his mind. The moment passed.
Reluctant sleepers sorely left their beds,
Not breaking but diminishing by steps.
Some cursed the cold, others bowed their heads
While from the fields huge banks of fog rolled up;
The dead were stirring, exhaling through the earth.

Prayer for the Harvest

Tomorrow may we all be light,
Blessed with second sight
That brings the world to us
As children understand it.
The sweet mare in her stall
Will be still enough for all
Of us who whisper our confessions.
Come evening may we sleep all night
In the crooked arm of Mother Time
Where the owl's vigil calms us,
Where the fox in the harrowed field thrills us.
Tomorrow may we all be right
In every thing we say and do,
Forgiving ourselves our dispositions,
And those who can't forgive us.

For Lysa, That She May Rise Early

Each morning between five and six
When twenty serious cows file out,
And the waking cries of sheep
Are the sweetest of the various sounds
That turn night into day,
The world's weather is most inhuman,
Though most secure.
One's apprehension disappears—
As if fog to some high ship ascends,
Mysterious as Prague,
As if you could become
One with the field itself,
And the motion of the animals.

The Sheep That Feeds You

Lower your face to the platter;
Breathe in the steam, my sweet essence
Mingling with the scent of your own sweat,
As intimate as coworkers crossing an unspoken line,
Or as killer and victim
In the exhilarating rush of opposing intentions.
Lose your senses in the smell of me ripened at last,
Exquisite after the stink of muddy fields. Remember?

All winter and spring you chased me down,
Grabbing among the hysterical flock
For a fist of my wool. You gathered me
To your chest, ignoring the pellets of shit
I let loose in protest (that smeared
the rain-slickered arm pinning a back leg),
And puckered some foreleg skin, hunting a vein
For the injection that fought off three kinds of death,
Or shot a thick solution down my throat
For a new rainbow of worms in my belly.

Did we ever find comfort in each others' eyes,
And did you imagine us coming to any end but this?

I was never troubled so, knowing only the day and night,
The security of the muddy field beneath my hooves,
The gradual, growing distance between my mother and me,
The late-calling, persistent sexual goad.
For my kind there is only the shepherd's truck
And his dog's incredible, hectoring speed,
Steel tubs filled with fresh water, and salt licks
Blessing a patch of dead ground. There is

Only the shade of the one pear tree on a blistering day,
Or the comfort of roof and warm hay in the barn
When it rains or snows, when the night is bitter.

I feel your confusion now that my ear tag's gone.
Which are you? you're thinking.
Is it you, 56? 43?
You know me. Put numbers out of your head.
Breathe deeply now we're together again under Heaven's bright eye.

Grateful

Be grateful that you live
Inside the head you do.
How many times have you
Gone sailing through
Your bed or favorite chair to
Wave a sign in the sleaze
Of traffic: *Need Money, Please!*

How many times have you
Suffered with the losers
Of war, or chafed and simmered
On a reservation, or brokered
The rescue of many from fear?
How many hours have you
Survived the lessons of gender

Change, or held your hero,
So splendid because of you?
Be grateful. Be father and mother,
Be teacher, sister, and brother
In all that you dream and do,
Against the day your ledger
Is opened up to you.

Travelers

Because we love the stars
We walk out late to gaze at them.
Because we love the night
We put it on and will not come away.
The stars, the night,
Are all the substance of our thought.
No suffering cries out,
No death comes near,
As time continues on its way,
Remote beneath the stars,
Inside the open night.

Quiet, Please

The quiet of a house
When all are asleep
Is more beautiful than sleep.
Tell that to the waitress
Dead on her feet.
Tell it to the caged
Cashier at the all-nite U-Pump.
Tell it to your ghost
Still running the Fleshing Machine
At the pre-dawn tannery.
Tell it to the firefighters,
Cops, and doorway sleepers.
Tell it to the animals.
Tell it tell it
Until you agree:
The quiet of a horse
Under a full moon
And a fragrant tree
Is more beautiful than you,
Than me.

Four Hundred Apples

The peeler slices through human skin
As easily as fruit skin.
A west-facing kitchen
In late afternoon sweats you,
And no matter what system you divine
The apples spin out of their jackets
In their own good time. But you
Would like to find more in the labor
Than the eventual sweetness of pies—
How, for example, to quiet compulsion,
Your need to be burning, even in water.
Mind the peeler, then the knife in your hand.
There are the apples, stripped and diced
In a syrup of brown sugar and Mexican vanilla.
The first part of the lesson is easy,
But part two always gives you trouble—
Eating the pies, and
While doing that, enjoying them.

Paranoid

His daughter's doll escapes
From a box on the table
And follows him to work
In her plastic car.
At day's end she's his shadow,
Frowning at items
He tosses into his basket
At the store.
He can't help watching in
The rearview mirror
As she touches up her lipstick
And jabs at her lashes
With a tiny brush.
Maybe he should wave her
Off the road,
Say to that all-night drive-in,
And buy her a Crush,
And attempt to pry out of her
The mysterious news—
Like what her boyfriend will do
If he sees them together;
Like what his daughter's up to
Out of his sight,
And why a dish like her
Is on his tail,
Always watching him.

Women and Men

Women understand:
Living with it so,
They master disappointment
Better than men,
Who never get the news,
Only its terror.

Living with it so,
Men disappear in cars,
Clubs, and bottles, inside
Their muddled heads,
While women turn on lights
And turn down beds,

And master the disappointment
That men are lost forever
In their fear. If only they
Could be more flexible,
Better in bed, more grace-
Ful in public.

That's the terror—
That men are almost useless,
That women's hearts may break
On their behalf, then must
Repair to build some peace,
Where men are nowhere.

Forgive Us Our Trespasses

On our national day of The Beggar
The President instructed the Secret Service
To admit to the White House grounds
One of the unfortunates holding a cap
Or tin cup out to passersby on Pennsylvania Avenue.
Two gate agents cracked jokes, selected a rag man
With flaming alcoholic skin. Inside their booth
They fed him moldy bread, gave him tepid water to drink,
Then laid him in a corner, wrapped in flea-infested blankets.

So we observe our day of penance, one agent said.

Little time had passed when they were distracted
From their surveillance screens by rhythmic
Murmurs coming from the heap on the floor.

Old man, one said, *what's that you're saying?*

But the man in the blanket continued, unbroken, his recitation.

It's weird, the other said. *I wish he'd stop.*

The agents tried talking over him
When ignoring him was impossible.
They gave him halfhearted kicks,
Then slumped down at their desks.
Suddenly one of them stood up.

I know! he cried. *The old man's talking poetry!*
Just then the President called the booth.

How is our guest? he asked.

He is cursing you and the nation in rhyme,
One of the agents answered.

There was little hesitation.
                                        Tomorrow,
The Chief Executive ordered, *the beggar*
shall be scourged at 10 a.m.
During a Rose Garden press conference,
Followed by his crucifixion on the South Lawn.

The next day, at the base of the stainless steel cross,
The beggar was asked if he had any last thing to say.

Only that we not delay, he replied.
I have fought in war, and all wars are evil.
I was your laureate and told the truth. I am
Content. My dream lived well, and now is done.

Nobody came to lay the body in a tomb.
By nightfall, crows had devoured the beggar's eyes.

FOUR

Brother, are you walking my way?

—*Paul Robeson*

Red Foxes

Insomnia pushed Nessa over the falls,
Her boat made of nothing but her own skin.
Deep in the comforter she curled like a baby
Waiting for sleep to return. Under the down
She willed herself a dream, but nothing came.
Nothing but cold and the prickly, pre-dawn stillness.
As fast as a ghost she stepped out of her sleeper,
Pulled on her woolen shirt and knee-high socks,
Her jeans and Red Wing boots. The glowing clock
Read three as Nessa hustled to the window
Above the field of young rye grass. The crop
Lay under the fog, straining toward warmer weather,
But winter always stayed too long. She tiptoed
Past her parents' room and down the stairs.
Nessa wondered how they could sleep tonight.

Bundled up in a coat, a hat and gloves,
She headed for the field beyond the barn
And longed for the voice to call her—
                                    "Come into the field
Where all of us are living out our time."

Instead, not very high up in the fog
She heard the staggered honks of migrating geese.
They reminded her of students on a bus
Who squirm and *yak yak yak* to steer the time.
And *did* the leader really know the way?
She shivered, thinking *I am not alone.*
Instinctively she angled left and saw
A low shape moving calmly through the mud.

Nessa slowed down, peering into the fog,
And met the red eyes glowing in the dark.

"I know you," Nessa said. "Lady Possum,
Your belly must be as empty as a can
For you to be prowling so late on this grumpy night."
She matched the possum's pace. "I wish you'd speak,"
She said, "if only to explain your eyes.
How come they're red in the dark? My cat's are yellow.
What color do you see when you look at mine?'

They paralleled each other up the fence line
To the corner where the possum disappeared
In the thicket growing round the apple trees
That Nessa's people abandoned years ago.
She watched the possum burrow out of sight
And thought about the buyers moving in.
Would they have children? *Odds are they'll be improvers,*
She told herself, *removing this nest of vines*
And driving out the birds and animals;
They might break up the farm to sell off lots . . . ,

Nessa darkened. *They might clear-cut the hill—*
Just like their neighbor down Gap Road, the one
Who never has a word for anyone
Even when spoken to. He puts down traps
For possum, stray cats, skunks, anything
That dares to live where he's put up a fence.
In Nessa's memory, hardly a week
Had passed without the stop-your-heart report
Of his rifle, and many times he'd need two rounds

(The second even worse, meaning he'd failed
To kill his victim with a single shot).

When she was younger Nessa shot a bird.
She was playing Annie Oakley. Her friend Ramon
Had handed her his Christmas BB gun.
She raised the barrel, sighting a mockingbird
On a telephone wire. "One shot," she told her friend.
Impossible. They both laughed at her bragging
As she squeezed the trigger, then the bird fell down.
Ramon picked up the rifle, ran for home,
While Nessa, unbelieving, held the bird,
Refusing to accept the death she'd made.
So that was how easy making death could be.

❦

While Nessa walked her father sat in his chair
Between the woodstove and east-facing window.
He felt his years in the hands that held the cup,
In his heart that beat too loudly in his head.

"The bankers must hold papers on the fog
As well as the farm," he told himself. "Damn them."

A sheet of damp wood sizzled in the stove
Then blistered and exploded, arcing through
The open doors to the carpet. William was slow
To move, and in that indecisive moment
Flared a crazy thought: *The house is old,
It's possible.* But sense (or habit) prevailed.
He stamped on the ember, smiling at little burns

That scarred the carpet, a map of almost-fires.
A door creaked open, draft of cold air struck.
"It's Daddy," William said. "I'm by the fire."

Nessa kissed his cheek. He touched her hair
As she laid her head on his chest. She smelled of fog.

"You've been out walking," he said. "Did you circle the field?"

She nodded, leaning back to look at him.

"Come, red fox, be my guardian," Nessa
Whispered, as she had so many times
At bedtime when her father told her stories
Of the woods and fields. "Come, red fox, be our guide."

William turned to the woodstove saying, "Our luck's
Run out. Nothing will lift us up today."

Then Nessa's eyes were wet. She wrapped her arms
Around her father's middle from behind,
Hugging so fiercely it took him by surprise,
His power escaping like water over stone.
Like fog rolling over ditches, she thought.
They stood together, silent, sharing that touch
Until a bell ringing set them both
In motion. William hung the woodstove screen;
Nessa shook out the wheelchair's blanket and pillow
As William climbed the stairs, and moments later
Came down again, holding his wife in his arms.

By then the auctioneer was soaking up
A streak of egg yolk with a wedge of rye.
The banker across the table skimmed the paper,
Impatient to go. The older man could read him.

"A minute," he said, "and two more maple bars."

He signaled the waitress, requesting one more coffee
For the road. "I've got to have that kick," he said.
The banker thought of his final college term,
Living on speed as he drove toward his degree.
Now his job was easier. The figures,
The plusses and minuses bracketing his life
Made feeling a cinch; he felt the bottom line.

The auctioneer was different, a local boy
And former football star at Central Linn;
But game days in the fifties were far away.
Twice married, supporting five kids in their teens,
He specialized in liquidating estates,
Making hard times harder, talking faster
To anaesthetize the crowd's collective thought.
Foreclosures were the worst. The night before
He always felt remorse, especially
If he knew the family. But experience
Had calmed him down. The victims on sell-off day
Would suffer their greatest grief, and then go on.
(Wasn't there a famous play like that?
He couldn't recall, his reading days remote.)
It was always the same. The family
Might watch till early afternoon, then leave.

The banker's sudden question made him laugh.
"Has anybody been shot at one of these?"

He picked his teeth. The auctioneer said *no*
And asked if he had ever seen the place.

"Not me. I see it when we sell it off.
Sometimes I wish I worked home loans instead,
But that gets messy, too. You get involved,
You know what I mean? And when the loan blows up
You feel responsible. That's not for me.

Nessa's mother smoothed the shawl on her legs
And stared at the fire. She drew a rattling breath
As if to say *I'm finished with this now.*

"Can I get you something, Momma?"

                                        "You've been in the field.
You saw them, then?" the older woman asked.

"I stumbled on a possum. I heard some geese,
But dark and fog were over everything.
I felt them in the shadows watching me,
But I didn't see them, no." Nessa wished
That for once she could have told a healing lie—

If only foxes carried us away,
Or wrapped a magic shawl around the farm—

She shook her head, facing the present once more,
And noticed her mother staring, far away.
"The fog has lifted a little," Nessa said.

❦

They picked at breakfast, listening to the drone
Of strangers working, setting up the yard.
The auctioneer's assistant shuffled in,
A clipboard in hand, a pencil behind one ear.

"Boss says we'll sell the tools and tractor first."

He spoke, not really to them but just to hear
A familiar sound. It kept him company.
It shielded him from the crippled woman's stare
(he felt for them, but hell, this was his job).
"Most folks are done by two o'clock," he said.
"So there's our window."
                              Nessa liked that thought—
A window that could suddenly be shut.

❦

The turnout was good. Men were there for tools;
Women picked over tables for smaller things—
Kitchen appliances, bedding, handmade clothes,
A chair admired at a social long ago.
Nessa knew the auction etiquette,
Her family's place. Even their neighbors would turn
Away from them, keeping their hands busy.
She knew her job: to make them feel less guilty.
Embarrassing? Of course, she told herself.

She had seen her shame and loss on other faces,
On other days. Now the things they loved changed hands.
Her mother's face was stony as the quilts
She'd made sold quickly at a modest price.
Antique dealers? Nessa guessed they were.
When a batch of her mother's dresses came on the block
She turned away.
                              Out to the barn she ran.
Standing in the empty, hay-sweet place,
Which looked so big with no machinery,
She traveled back, remembering the summer
Her father and his friend had wrestled beams
Of pressure-treated lumber into place,
Restoring a foundation so delicate
It seemed a gust of wind might flatten it.
And once, while Nessa watched, the jack that held
A section up collapsed, the roof descending
Three feet or so, but holding as the two
Men in the loft yelled out in fear, then laughed
To see the roof intact, themselves alive.

But now her senses told her *look around.*
Stepping soundlessly to the rough-cut door
Of a small side room, she saw in its dusty light
Her father hauling a strongbox out of the ground.
William looked younger than she knew him to be.

It's money, enough to save us,
                              she heard him say
Though he did not speak. A rain cloud covered the sun,

And in that purple light the man with his booty
Went into the air like smoke on a damp burn day.

"I'm breathing too much of this barn's old fevered air,"
She said, but there the fox stood at the door.
Then girl and animal traveled into each other
As far as they could, into the spirit's house
Where the red fox said,

                       "Into the world we're born,
Then out we're called again. Go back to your people.
They're calling you like foxes call up the night."

Then he was gone, but Nessa could hear the voice
As she ran back to the heat of the furious sale.
Her mother was already seated in the Ford
While William stood off by the oak tree with a friend.
She caught his eye, he broke free with a nod.
"I'm ready now," she said.

                       They backed away
From house and barn, quiet in memory,
As the crowd around the auctioneer closed ranks,
Shutting them out, glad to see them going.

Southwest, then west by Courtney Creek they drove,
The trailer like a pendulum behind.
They stared, not at the fields around them, but
At years behind them. The sky filled up with clouds.
A soft rain fell as William hit the lights.

They had nowhere to go, only relations
In Washington who could put them up for a spell.
They'd look for a rental, maybe a doublewide
On a farm where one or more of them could work.
William squinted, wiping at windshield mist
With the back of his sleeve.

                        "Stop!" his wife commanded.
She had seen them first, the bareheaded man and his dog
Who were walking without baggage down the road.
Perhaps the man had put his car in the ditch
And needed help, she thought. Somehow she knew
He wasn't homeless, and even if he were,
What did it matter? They were homeless, too.
They slowed to a crawl, and William spoke to the man.

"It's wet out there. You'd better ride with us."

The stranger nodded, climbed in back with Nessa.
His dog, a tri-color sheltie, sat between them.
Nessa looked them over. Her first impression
Was that the man was young, but now she saw
She couldn't really tell how old he was.
The man looked fit. His eyes and face were good,
So she stroked his dog, who leaned on her for more.

"He looks a little like a fox," she said.

"That's so," the man agreed. It's then she noticed
His eyes were like the dog's, like eyes she'd seen
So many times in the fields, out in the dark.
"He's always been my guide," he said, and smiled.

Nessa's mother turned to look at them.
"It's funny you should put it that way," she said,
"Especially today." Her daughter trembled.

"So where you headed?" William's nervous eyes
In the mirror were on the stranger.
                                        "Nowhere," he said.
"It doesn't really matter where I go;
What counts is how I make out while I get there.
Each day there's something new to lift us up.
Today we needed help, and there you were."

"Yes," the woman in the front seat said.
"That's how it was." She reached for William's hand
And movement out the window caught her eye.
Beyond the stranger's shoulder, in the field
She saw two foxes running easily,
Paralleling their car.
                                  Then all were watching,
The dog as well, as Nessa smoothed his hair.
The foxes ran and ran until they vanished
In the longer grasses bordering the field.
At the interstate the travelers were calm,
Even grateful as they found their way.

FIVE

Blessings to them, my pony, who used to run and sit with us.

—*Liam Rector, "My Pony"*

The Islander

*After Tomás O'Crohán, chronicler of the
Great Blasket Island, whose last human
residents were removed in 1953.*

When I move off my island
Winter will go with me,
Our names in the sand
Disfigured by the sea.
The wind will blow
Where my people go.

Great storms bull through our houses,
Time flattens the seawall.
A songbird browses
In the ass-deserted stall.
How could we know
Where our world would go?

Like rags for the poor we're gathered,
Like crockery we break.
Who among us bothered
To prepare for this heartache,
This final blow
On the world we know?

No Blasket man is free
Of the politician's scheme.
What trick of cruelty
Makes me the last to dream?
May my curragh repair,
Never sailing from there.

Give us this day our portion,
Which is salty, small, and dry.
The pride of our nation
Is water in the eye.
The wind will blow
Where my people go.

The Banshee, riding a cloud,
Gathers my thoughts tonight
In her winding shroud.
May stories told by firelight
Survive in the air,
An echo there.

The wind will blow
Through the world we know,
Where my people go.

A Prayer to You

Each night I get down on my knees and pray,
And though I start with God I come to you,
Your name and face before the things I seek.
I turn away, but turning, I still pray
That you will write to me, not like a speech
Or like a sister of the Blessed Virgin,
But as you are: Laughing like the rapids,
Unmatched in the magic of words, fearless
In the glare of time, lovelier than morning.
And when that animal that would eat us all
Appears, regarding us from the corners of
His jealous eyes, together we might end
His misery. Reproachful, sympathetic,
Come back for me. Your Robert, your fanatic.

Emily's Courtship

The visitor stands at the grave in knee-high snow.
He's been calling your house since 1962
Asking for you.

Is he a distant or close relation to
That man in Baltimore who annually visits Poe?
Certainly you would know.

And if this man who calls you should break through,
What loneliness, time and pain must he endure
At your father's door?

Brushing aside that meddling sister of yours,
He calls upstairs, "Emily, my darling, my dear,
There is nothing to fear!"

Don't greet him in the frills and curls you acquired late,
Long after the Romantics claimed you,
But come down as you

Always were, your hair tucked in a tight bun,
Your limbs loose in a drab, light summer dress
The color of afternoon sun,

The armpits and a flare up the back darkened with sweat
(for you have been sweeping all morning), Your shoes
Dusty, impossibly small.

Come down to the parlor, dear, and rest.
Don't talk around the corner like a ghost,
Or too sly a host;

That ploy worked well enough on disabled Higginson,
And on ancient Wadsworth, so stiff with God
He couldn't bend.

Do not descend in a cloud of impossible cadences
And punctuation like slaps to the face—this one is yours,
All man and boy, your poetry toy

Who loves your jokes, and your laughter
Like water lapping in Heaven,
Who would take you as you are.

Still you test his devotion, serving him the heavy cake
You made from scratch the night (or the half-century?) before;
Your sister returns, the bore.

Sipping bitter tea she claims each word you say,
Or worse, presumes to say them *for* you.
That just won't do!

Your caller whispers in her ear, "Get lost! Your Sis and I
Need time alone, comprende?" With your taste for the exotic,
The far away you'll never see,

That single, foreign word rings like a wedding bell.
You shoo your flesh and blood away,
If only for a day.

Elegy in August

Sleep, little sister, far from pain.
Water smooths out stones in the river
As memory calms the chaos
You left behind. Rest easy, sister,
Your babies are older than you ever were.
Even the stain will fade
When none are left to remember
The calls for help you never made.

After burning, blackberry bushes
Struggle up through ash, and love, resilient,
Blooms in all seasons, even for you
Who suffered and could not tell what was right
As you hurled yourself, suddenly
Spiraling upward to darkness or light.

Daughter

—for Jane Mary Katherine

This is the day
You come away
With us, meeting
Face to face
The committee greeting
Your arrival. You rush
From acrobatic sleep

On this the day
Your parents say
Thank God! or words
To that effect.
They are skittish as birds
Of the architect
You spring out of.

Jane, you begin this day
To break away
From your cozy zoo
And our busybody,
Good-intentioned say
About all the things
In store for you.

This is the day,
And this the hour
When all is still
But the rain shower,
And the close-up murmur
Of your parents' prayer
As you join us there.

The Moon through the Trees

The eyes of animals shine in the grass,
Skunk silver, possum red. Far out
From the Northwest corner, your house

With its lighted windows looks
Like a ship at sea. You almost
Hear voices singing *Nearer My God to Thee*

When a green light appears, as dazzling as
The flash that blinds, then fills you
With sight, then goes with a head-on look.

It's the owl's eyes burning down from the barn's cupola,
It's the moon through the trees spreading itself
On the red fox emerging from midnight thickets.

It's the sight of the dead, the mural
Of your past, the teasing glimpse
Of what comes when you are no one.

The Discovery

Under the feeder
Not far away
We found her dead,
The cat, Go Away.

The cat, Go Away,
Our Three Oaks tart
On a mound of seed,
A beak in her heart.

The beak had a message
Pushed back on its base:
Death to stalkers!
Thus ends the chase.

We nervously scouted
The air all that day,
But the hit-bird got her—
Our cat, Go Away.

This Time of Year

The world practices death.
Our valley fills up with wind and rain
While we who are too poor to have insulation
Have already sealed our windows with plastic sheets;
Blurring the world, we miss our dearly departed.
It's what we deserve, but some
More evenly suggest this life is simply benign
Repetition, a grander scheme than we can know.
The dead lie deep and cold.
Our rehearsals never seem to end,
And our little prayers for summer go up.
A woman of eighty rubs her legs,
A man of forty mimics her.
A child rubbing the sleep from his eyes
Wishes his warmer dreams still held him.
Back to houses the cats come faster
From ditches, gardens, haunted barns,
While sheep, pathetic, scrabble in fields
baa baa baaing—for what?
To come indoors, perhaps to be cats.

Far, and Near

When I am low as the coast range darkens,
I remember the things I can count on:
The weather, some sticks and stones,
The circuit of cows; headlights of a pick-up
Chugging down a steep gravel road;
Two crows scanning the orchard,
Alighting for the magic hour
On the windmill's still blade;
Myself, thinking anything I choose.
Or more to the point, inhabited by
Any thought or image that chooses me.

Tonight I am over there on horseback,
With you on the road beside me.
I lean down, the reins light in my left hand,
And hold out my right arm, which you,
With little coaxing, take hold of.
You swing up on the saddle in front of me
As easily as a girl.
The valley lights come on for us like stranded stars.
I close my knees, feeling your back press into me.
Then we are going, you, me, and Bridey
To the hill where I hope we'll find
That lifting of the spirit I always feel there.
The night wind is fragrant with your hair;
It is the voice of all creation saying

Do you hear it? Can you feel us? Do you see?

There, or not there. Once
You went out riding with me
To a place where two are always we.

Dana, Her Eyes

I want to live in there
Where light is so calm and clear
The moon must have a hand in it;
Where all the locks in my head
Spring open like the jaw set in
The body's old belief that nothing
As beautiful as long-looking into her eyes
Would ever be its fate; where
Our house, somewhere in a clearing
Opens its rooms of unusual intimacy;
Where spirit-stuff, like the magic dust
Of stars, supercharges sex. Always
I want that oddball sensation, giddy,
Toppling, out of balance for a moment,
Then out of pain for the rest of my life.

Prayers That Open Heaven

Of a declaration of faith proclaimed among many,
The congregation rising up in song;
Of a lonesome walk around a muddy pasture,
A lullaby boating children to sleep;
Of the bond between your dog and you,
Of forgiveness for those who burn fields
And break promises, who use their power
To lord it over others; of the ditch you dig
With a neighbor, the piles of leaves you rake,
The barn's sure bridge to the past;
Of Our Father and Hail Mary,
Of the sight of a solitary rider
In late afternoon sun on the Cascade range,
The horse moving like the motion of God;
Of a sky so full of stars you know you are not alone.
What are the prayers that open Heaven, where
Are the words and guides you should follow?
No one answers, no one lifts up your heart but you.

NOTES

This book is dedicated to Dana Gerhardt and our children, Dylan, Eoghan, Branden, and Jane.

All of the poems with country settings take place on and around a small seed grass farm in the Willamette Valley in central Oregon, and horse country outside Ashland.

"There Is": The Northwest's salmon population is making a comeback. Clear-cutting, the process by which an entire hillside of trees can be reduced to stumps in a matter of days, is a hot issue argued between the logging interests and those who oppose the practice. Blue herons are beautiful. They are also notorious for fishing clean a stocked pond.

"My Eastern Friend" is for Liam Rector.

"Sisters" is based on a family I was told many stories about when I lived in the Mojave Desert in the mid-seventies.

"The Pact" may or may not be a true story. It depends on which local legends you choose to believe around Brownsville, Halsey, and Sweet Home, Oregon. The hundred-year-old barn *is* real; it was restored to its original condition between 1989 and 1998 with the help of Paul Baxter, Joseph Bednarik, and Bruce McMurray. This poem is for Lysa McDowell, and our neighbors.

"The Sheep That Feeds You": For two years we ran sheep with a neighbor, until we couldn't stand it anymore (the sheep, not the neighbor). It is interesting

that when people run sheep, it is many years—if ever—
until they can eat lamb again. This poem is for Farmer
Larry, Larry Pearl.

"Forgive Us Our Trespasses" was inspired by several
Irish legends.

"Red Foxes" is a conversion story. We joined the
Catholic church in Ireland after our son, Eoghan Patrick
Morgan, was born there in the spring of 1992.

"The Islander": The stories of Tomás O'Crohán were
collected in two volumes printed in Ireland, *The
Islandman*, and *Island Cross-Talk*. He is one of the great
storytellers of the twentieth century.

"Elegy in August" is for Beverly Anne McDowell, who
died at age 35 in 1980.

"Daughter": This poem is for my daughter, born 16
January 1997, and her godparents, Mary and Dana
Gioia.

ACKNOWLEDGMENTS

Grateful acknowledgement is made to the following publications where these poems first appeared, sometimes in earlier versions:

Boulevard: "October"; *Connecticut Review*: "The Valley of the In-Betweens"; *The Hudson Review*: "After," "Far and Near," "My Eastern Friend," "The Moon through the Trees," "The Pact," "Red Foxes," "Surprise," "There Is," "Travelers"; *Janus*: "Paranoid"; *Poetry*: "Elegy in August"; *Poetry New York*: "Four Hundred Apples"; *Sycamore Review*: "For Lysa, That She May Rise Early"; *The Formalist*: "My Bird, Your Face"; *The Kenyon Review*: "Sisters"; *The Little Magazine*: "The Fleshing Machine"; *The New Criterion*: "Emily's Courtship," "Where and What You Are"; *The Sewanee Review*: "The Islander," "Prayers That Open Heaven," "Prayer for the Harvest"; *Solo*: "Levels of Intersection."

"The Pact" was published in a special limited edition, and "Daughter" as a broadside, by Michael Peich's Aralia Press.

"Grateful" was published in *Place of Passage: Contemporary Catholic Poetry* by Story Line Press.

The author thanks Kim Addonzio, Lynn Freed, Mark Jarman, Maxine Kumin, Frederick Morgan, Louis Simpson, Chase Twitchell, the readers, editors, and publishers above, and the staff of the University of Pittsburgh Press for their kindness and encouragement.

ROBERT MCDOWELL is the author two previous books of poetry, *The Diviners* (1995), a book-length poem, and *Quiet Money* (1987). He is the co-author, with Mark Jarman, of *The Reaper Essays* (1996), and, with Harvey Gross, of *Sound and Form in Modern Poetry* (1995). The editor of two anthologies, *Poetry After Modernism* and *Cowboy Poetry Matters*, and the co-translator of Ota Pavel's *How I Came to Know Fish*, McDowell has published essays, reviews, poems, and fiction in numerous journals and anthologies in the United States and internationally. He is the founding publisher and editor of Story Line Press.